POPULAR IRISH SONGS

Edited by

Florence Leniston

DOVER PUBLICATIONS, INC., New York

Copyright © 1992 by Dover Publications, Inc.
All rights reserved under Pan American and International Copyright Conventions.

This Dover edition, first published in 1992, is a new selection of songs originally published by various publishers, 1808–1914. (Publishing information for each song appears in the table of contents.) The introduction was specially written for this edition.

We are grateful to the New York Public Library, the Library of Congress, the Free Library of Philadelphia, Sandy Marrone and Larry Zimmerman for providing several of these song sheets for reproduction.

Manufactured in the United States of America
Dover Publications, Inc., 31 East 2nd Street, Mineola, N.Y. 11501

Library of Congress Cataloging-in-Publication Data

Popular Irish songs / edited by Florence Leniston.
     1 score.
  Reprints. Originally published 1808–1914 (various publishers).
  For voice and piano.
  ISBN 0-486-26755-5 (pbk.)
    1. Popular music—Ireland. 2. Popular music—United States. 3. Irish Americans—Music. I. Leniston, Florence.
M1745.18.P66 1992   91-759444
                                               CIP
                                                M

CONTENTS

INTRODUCTION

THE SONGS in this volume represent a selection of the best and best-known from the song traditions—folk, salon and popular—of Ireland and of England and America insofar as they deal with Irish subjects.

For almost two centuries, Irish music has been widely regarded as one of the great folk repertories of the world. The Irish harp, recalling the bardic tradition of the Irish harpers that continued unbroken from the Middle Ages to the early nineteenth century, has been the island's symbol for almost 500 years. The heritage of Irish folk music perhaps first took concrete form in a collection published in Dublin around 1726, and many more followed in the succeeding decades.

The surge in romantic feeling near the turn of the century, with its exalting of the spirit of the folk, had led Robert Burns to provide new lyrics to hundreds of Scottish folk tunes, and in 1807 an English publisher commissioned a young Irish poet and songwriter, Thomas Moore (1779–1852), to do the same with the repertory of Irish folk melodies. Moore's *A Selection of Irish Melodies*, with musical arrangements by John Stevenson (1761–1833), was published between 1808 and 1834, eventually totaling some 130 songs. The refined and handsome Moore was himself his songs' greatest advocate; he sang them in his sweet tenor at the piano in the salons of England and Ireland, moving his audiences to tears. The songs achieved an amazingly broad dissemination in the course of the century. Trailing their auras of melancholy, nostalgia, historical reverie, gentle grief, lovelorn yearning—and occasional high spirits, though never comedy—they embodied the purest romantic emotions and became touchstones of romantic expression.

These strains are heard in Moore's successors as well. The midcentury Irish song is represented in this collection by "Molly Bawn," "The Rose of Tralee," "Kathleen Mavourneen," "Killarney" and "Come Back to Erin."

The great famine of 1845–51 sent nearly a million Irish to America, where many settled in the large Northern cities. It was not long before a lore began to collect around the Irish immigrant community and their magically beautiful island homeland. The public delight in things Irish coincided with the tremendous growth of the American sheet-music industry in those same cities.

Homesickness, humor, boisterousness and love—never tragedy or political strife—were the hallmarks of the Irish-American popular song, which maintained a large presence in North America for about 75 years. Musically it was unrelated to Irish folk music, and hardly distinguishable from the other hits of the time. Its popularity probably peaked around 1890, with a smaller, "second-generation"

peak around 1912 and later a fondly retrospective swell in the 1940s.

In recent decades, fine new repertories of Irish song have been rediscovered and newly composed. But the older repertory—of which millions of Americans of every ethnic background in, say, 1920 could sing almost every line—survives on its own great merits and today forms a significant part of the American musical heritage.

THE BAND PLAYED ON (1895). John F. Palmer, a New York actor, was this song's original author; Charles B. Ward, its publisher, apparently made only small contributions but did sing it successfully on the vaudeville stage. Though Palmer claimed it was inspired by a *German* street band, the lyric's details give it a strong Irish flavor. Its sheet-music sales eventually amounted to over a million copies.

BELIEVE ME, IF ALL THOSE ENDEARING YOUNG CHARMS (1808). This famous melody may date back to the 1730s, when it was apparently heard in a London ballad opera. It is still unknown where in the British Isles the tune originated. With the words "My Lodging Is on the Cold Ground" it was sung in Sheridan's *The Rivals* in 1775. But the modern version had to wait until 1808, when Thomas Moore published his own touching lyric in his *Irish Melodies*. Yet another poem was underlaid in 1836 on the occasion of Harvard University's 200th year, and "Fair Harvard" became its official alma mater.

COME BACK TO ERIN (1866). Charlotte Alington Barnard (1830–69) was an Englishwoman who chose to write her many popular songs under the fairylike pseudonym of Claribel (probably borrowed from Tennyson's poem of the same name). This one was the most successful of all; with its characteristically Irish turns of phrase, it has often been thought to be a folk song. "Mavourneen" means "my darling," and "Aroon" means "darling."

DANNY BOY (1913). The "Londonderry Air" (or "Air from County Derry") was called by the English composer Sir Hubert Parry the most beautiful melody ever written, and many have seconded him in scarcely less effusive terms. It was first collected and published in 1855, without title or words, and the identity of its inspired composer has never been ascertained. It soon acquired the lyrics "My Gentle Harp" (by Thomas Moore) and "Would God I Were the Tender Apple Blossom" (by Katherine Hinkson), and in 1913 Fred Weatherly recreated it as "Danny Boy," in which form it became a great hit on both sides of the Atlantic.

DOWN WENT MCGINTY (1889). At a time when the Irish theme was at its peak, this novelty ballad became perhaps the most popular American song of its year. Joe Flynn was half of an Irish variety act, and he obviously envisioned a broadly physical skit to accompany the song's performance. The drinking, brawling and general haplessness depicted were the lot of the comic Irishman of the era. But the song's humor is less than uproarious, and its great popularity remains surprising.

DRILL, YE TARRIERS, DRILL (1888). This lusty tune sounds as though it was indeed written by a tarrier, or Irish excavation worker. Thomas Casey was a tarrier himself, who also sang at local political clubs and music halls such as Tony Pastor's, but he may not have actually written the song. Its modal seventh degree suggests Irish folk music. The spoken line after each stanza indicates the song's stage possibilities. (The reference to the *Staats-Zeitung*, New York's German newspaper, is a reminder of the other great wave of immigrants that arrived with the Irish.)

THE HARP THAT ONCE THROUGH TARA'S HALLS (1808). The Hill of Tara in County Meath, near Dublin, was the seat of the ancient Irish kings. This tune, titled "Gramachree," first appeared in a Scottish collection of 1746, but it is quite possible that it was brought to Scotland by Irish harpers. It was sung with the words "Will You Go to Flanders" before Thomas Moore wrote his poem for it in 1807. Though Moore had many friends among the Irish nationalists, he did not write true resistance songs—unless a song such as this can be considered one.

HARRIGAN (1907). George M. Cohan (1878–1942) dominated the American musical stage in the early years of the century. Though American-born and a great patriot, his lineage was Irish and he enjoyed himself with Irish themes. "Harrigan" was first heard in *Fifty Miles from Boston*, his successful show of 1908. But it is James Cagney's rendition in his indelible performance as Cohan in the 1942 movie *Yankee Doodle Dandy* that lingers in the American memory. The song was Cohan's own tribute to Ned Harrigan (see "The Mulligan Guard").

HAS ANYBODY HERE SEEN KELLY? (1909). This song began life in a version popular in the English music hall by C. W. Murphy and Will Letters, "Kelly from the Isle of Man." For the American market, William McKenna (1881–1950) changed the geographical references, among other things, but in doing so left the story somewhat confused. What is an unmarried Irish couple doing crossing the Atlantic together in 1909? And does Kelly's straying convey any implication of infidelity—apparently the intention of the original? But no such quibbles interfered with the song's success, which was ensured by Nora Bayes's vivid comic performances.

I'LL TAKE YOU HOME AGAIN, KATHLEEN (1876). Like "The Band Played On," this song is not quite specifically Irish, but the implication is very strong, and the lyric probably aroused nostalgic pining in millions of Americans who had never seen the Emerald Isle. Thomas P. Westendorf (1848?–1923) was an Indiana schoolteacher, who took his inspiration from a friend's recent song, "Barney, Take Me Home Again."

I'VE GOT RINGS ON MY FINGERS (1909). Like several other songs in this collection, this one might not pass muster with the ethnically sensitive—but then, scrupulous an-thropology was never the domain of the American popular song. (The lyric has, however, been revised through the years.) Blanche Ring introduced it in *The Midnight Sons*, and then interpolated it into three more of her musicals, and this happy South Seas nonsense somehow made itself welcome everywhere. R. P. Weston, F. J. Barnes and Maurice Scott had no other significant hits together, but Weston cowrote the music-hall standard "I'm Henery the Eighth, I Am."

KATHLEEN MAVOURNEEN (1837). Despite centuries of political strife between them, the English were by no means immune to the charms of Ireland. Before moving to America in 1849, Frederick Crouch (1808–96) was a well-known English songwriter who often chose Irish themes. The "Mrs. Crawford" whose words he set is never correctly identified today. But in a newspaper interview Crouch stated that she was Mrs. Marion Crawford, a poet whose work sometimes appeared in the *Metropolitan Magazine*. There Crouch found "Kathleen Mavourneen" while lounging on the grass by Endesley Castle, Devonshire, in the summer of 1837, and immediately wrote his famous melody. The two subsequently met and collaborated further.

THE KERRY DANCE (1879). James Lyman Molloy (1837–1909), who would later write "Love's Old Sweet Song," hailed from County Offaly rather than County Kerry. He seems to have borrowed most of his melody from Margaret Casson's song "The Cuckoo," published in England around 1790. In style it resembles a fiddle tune, which may have suggested the subject of dancing to Molloy, who supplied a new middle section as well as entirely new words.

KILLARNEY (1862). Michael William Balfe (1808–70), the Irish composer and singer, was the most successful composer of English opera of the last century. He arranged fifty of Moore's Irish Melodies, and also wrote a number of individual songs, of which his very last, "Killarney," has always been the best known. His sometime librettist Edmund Falconer—the pen name of Edmund O'Rourke (1813–79)—wrote the lyric for his play *Innisfallen*.

LITTLE ANNIE ROONEY (1889). The irresistible swing of the chorus made "Little Annie Rooney" the biggest sheet-music hit of its time and a great perennial barroom singalong number. When he wrote it, Michael Nolan was an Irish entertainer performing in English music halls and Annie was his three-year-old cousin. (It is said that Nolan was so dismayed at the piracy of the song by American publishers that he never wrote another.)

A LITTLE BIT OF HEAVEN (1914). This trifle has shown a surprising resilience through the years. It was a thoroughly American product: J. Keirn Brennan (1873–1948) filled his lyric with every bit of Irish kitsch that came to mind, and Ernest R. Ball (1878–1927) matched it with a melody worthy of the words. The redoubtable trouper Chauncey Olcott (1860–1932) introduced it in the Irish musical *The Heart of Paddy Whack*.

MACUSHLA (1910). The authors of this song, Josephine V. Rowe and Dermot Macmurrough, had no other popular success. But "Macushla" was so successful that its name was borrowed for a hit Ernest Ball musical in 1914. The great classical tenor John McCormack, this century's most acclaimed singer of the Irish repertory, gave it and many popular hits of its kind a greater respectability through his performances and recordings.

THE MINSTREL BOY (1813). One of the most beautiful of all Irish songs, "The Minstrel Boy" is also an example of Thomas Moore's gently expressed sympathies with the Irish resistance to English rule, the minstrel's harp being the unmistakable symbol of Ireland. The lyric's discretion is such, however, that it could be sung with impunity in English drawing rooms. The lovely melody was originally called "The Moreen," according to Moore, but, astonishingly, no earlier printing of it has ever been found.

MOLLY BAWN (1841). The Irishman Samuel Lover (1797–1868) was a writer, songwriter and painter, as well as the grandfather of Victor Herbert. His other songs included "The Low-Backed Car" and "The Girl I Left Behind Me." *Il Paddy Whack in Italia*, in which the song first appeared, was a burlesque of Italian opera. (The Irishman was obviously grist for even the Irish humorist's mill long before he was a fixture of New York life.) "Bawn" is Irish for "fair."

MOLLY MALONE (ca. 1850?). Almost nothing is known of the origins of this justly famous song. It apparently incorporates one of the actual vendors' musical street cries with which Dublin's markets and alleys resounded for centuries. Composers had long incorporated them into their own music, and some became nursery rhymes ("Hot Cross Buns"). An actual nineteenth-century cry—in triple meter, like this one—went "Cockles and mussels alive! All alive! All alive! Fine fresh cockles!"

MOTHER MACHREE (1910). Even in an era that doted on "mother" songs, this paragon of sentiment stood out. Ernest Ball, Chauncey Olcott and Rida Johnson Young (1869–1926)—all Americans—collaborated on it for their Irish show *Barry of Ballymore*, and John McCormack later made it virtually his signature song. "Machree" means "my heart" or "my dear."

THE MULLIGAN GUARD (1873). The great minstrel and vaudeville team of Ned Harrigan (1845–1911) and Tony Hart (1855–91)—worthy of their own chapter in any history of American musical theater—gave birth to an entire genre with their staging of "The Mulligan Guard," written by Harrigan and David Braham (1838–1905). This infectiously buoyant march is a rare testament to an odd feature of big-city life in the later nineteenth century—what Sigmund Spaeth calls "the pseudo-military organizations that lingered after the [civil] war, giving militant die-hards and would-be soldiers a chance to wear some sort of uniform long after such exhibitionism had lost all patriotic significance." Such groups often attached themselves to politicians, providing a campaign with music and panoply. The Mulligan cadre paraded through the Lower East Side of Manhattan, historically a home to recent immigrants.

MY WILD IRISH ROSE (1899). Chauncey Olcott was one of the most popular singers, actors and songwriters of his time. Though born Chancellor John Olcott in Buffalo, New York, he came to represent the essence of Irishness on the New York stage. He made hits of many songs that were written for him, but this one, from his Irish show *A Romance of Athlone*, was easily the greatest success of those he wrote by himself, and it gave its title to his 1947 screen biography.

OFT IN THE STILLY NIGHT (1818). Thomas Moore included this song in the first volume of *A Selection of Popular National Airs*, calling the tune a "Scottish air." The only widely famous song from this collection, it is often assumed to have belonged to the *Irish Melodies*. The "Scotch snap" is heard several times in the melody. Abraham Lincoln particularly loved the song.

PEG O' MY HEART (1913). This song took its title from a popular nonmusical play, and seems to have won a competition for writing a song with that name. But in venerable hitmaking style, the lyric makes the eponymous Peg into an interchangeable love object. The German-born Fred Fischer (1875–1942)—later Fisher—was by now an established songwriter, and the Canadian Alfred Bryan (1871–1948) was another. The song was a modest success in the Ziegfeld Follies of 1913 but only when revived in 1947 and later did it reach the heights of success.

THE PRETTY GIRL MILKING HER COW (1796). Moore published this tune in 1813 with the words "The Valley Lay Smiling Before Me," but he would have first encountered the song in Gaelic, or in a risqué English version with this title. Bawdy enough to seem positively un-Irish, it was soon altered to the present lyric, which has since remained the most familiar.

THE ROSE OF TRALEE (ca. 1845). Little has been written about this song, and it has been given widely differing dates. Charles Glover (1806–63) was an English violinist and songwriter and musical director of the Queen's Theatre. John McCormack sang "The Rose of Tralee" in the film *Song o' My Heart* (1930).

SWEET ROSIE O'GRADY (1896). The only song ever credited to Maude Nugent (1877–1958), this very professional effort may actually have been written by her songwriter husband, William Jerome (1865–1932). Though publishers repeatedly passed it up, Nugent made it a hit through her own performances—but it is Annie Hart, most unjustly, whose picture appears on this edition. A true perennial, its title would reappear in other songs and on a Betty Grable film (1943), and two Manhattan bars still bear Rosie's name.

THROW HIM DOWN MCCLOSKEY (1890). The rawness of this narrative of New York low life could rarely have been equaled in the annals of popular song. But it made for perhaps the greatest hit of 1890, when Irish subjects were almost surefire. It was the biggest of several hits by John W. Kelly, a millworker turned songwriter. He wrote it for the 230-pound Maggie Cline, who belted it out (along with "Drill, Ye Tarriers, Drill") to tremendous effect in the New York music halls for many years.

'TIS THE LAST ROSE OF SUMMER (1813). This beautiful melody, which may date from the seventeenth century, bore the title "The Groves of Blarney" when Moore chose it for his new lyric. Beethoven, Mendelssohn and others used it as the basis for extended piano pieces, and Friedrich Flotow borrowed it for his opera *Martha*. The parlor tenor and the touring soprano took it up with equal fervor. Perhaps no other song of its century so captured the public's heart.

TOO-RA-LOO-RA-LOO-RAL (1913). In the movie *Going My Way* (1944) Bing Crosby made this song his own and brought it its greatest success, and many of his fans took it for either a folk lullaby or a newly written song. But it had actually been introduced by Chauncey Olcott in the 1914 revue *Shameen Dhu* (Black-haired Jimmy), and its American-born author, James Royce Shannon (1881–1946), could adopt a popular notion of black speech, for a song like "The Missouri Waltz," as easily as he could work the Irish vein.

THE WEARING OF THE GREEN (1865). The shamrock has been an Irish national symbol since before 1775, and its symbolic use was at least discouraged by the English. The wearing of green was never forbidden in any other sense, nor was the shamrock forbidden to grow; here these are, of course, metaphors for the impossibility of repressing nationalist feeling. This melody seems to date back to at least the 1830s and may be Scottish in origin. The lyric, apparently by the Irish-born playwright Dion Boucicault (1820?–90) and certainly sung in his play *Arrah Na Pogue*, is an adaptation of an earlier lyric from the turn of the century. A version of the later resistance song "The Rising of the Moon" employs the same tune.

WHEN IRISH EYES ARE SMILING (1912). This Irish-American anthem, the perennial theme of convivial gatherings, was yet another of Ernest Ball's great Irish hits, written with George Graff (1886–1973) and Chauncey Olcott and introduced by Olcott in his Irish musical *The Isle o' Dreams*. Though American-born, Ball was so devoted to Ireland that his screen biography (1944) was given the title of this song.

WHEN JOHNNY COMES MARCHING HOME (1863). The genesis of this stirring song is murky. The words at least were probably written by the Irish-born bandmaster and impresario Patrick Gilmore (1829–92) as the American Civil War raged. ("Louis Lambert" was apparently a nom de plume.) It has often been claimed that the melody is a folk tune from any of several countries, Ireland among them, but no published version before 1863 has ever been found. (The grimly antiwar Irish song "Johnny, I Hardly Knew Ye," which suggests a harsh parody of Gilmore's song, seems to postdate it, and probably only adopted the same melody at an even later date.) Widely sung during the Civil War and the Spanish-American War, "When Johnny Comes Marching Home" remains one of the finest songs of the entire American tradition.

WHERE THE RIVER SHANNON FLOWS (1905). A raft of hoary but harmless Irish clichés comes floating down the Shannon in this lyric. By 1905 hundreds of such songs were being written to an obvious commercial formula. James Russell teamed up with his brother John as a theatrical act.

WHO THREW THE OVERALLS IN MISTRESS MURPHY'S CHOWDER? (1898). Highly popular with Irish vaudevillians at the beginning of the century, this song has, in the decades since, continued to delight schoolchildren especially with its anarchic attitude toward food. The 1943 movie *Coney Island* gave it a new lease on life. George Geifer wrote no other hits and has remained otherwise unknown.

DEDICATED TO THE

New York Sunday World.

The
BAND
PLAYED ON

WORDS BY

JOHN F. PALMER.

MUSIC BY

Chas. B. Ward.

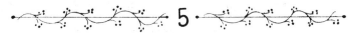

5

Published by

THE NEW-YORK MUSIC CO.,

57 WEST 28TH ST. NEW-YORK.

CHAS. SHEARD & CO LONDON. ENGL.

THE BAND PLAYED ON.

Words by
JOHN F. PALMER.

Music by
CHARLES B. WARD.

pay day came a - round each week they greased the floor with wax. And
Ca - sey was the fa - vor - ite and he that ran the ball. Of
thank'd them ver - y kind - ly for the fa vors they had shown. Then he'd

danced with noise and vig - or at the ball, _____ Each
kiss - ing and love - mak - ing did his share, _____ At
waltz once with the girl that he loved best. _____ Most

Sat - ur - day you'd see them dressed up in Sun - day clothes, Each
twelve o - clock ex - act - ly they all would fall in line, Then
all the friends are mar - ried that Ca - sey used to know, And

lad would have his sweet-heart by his side.____ When Ca - sey led the
march down to the din - ing hall and eat.____ But Ca - sey would not
Ca - sey too has tak - en him a wife.____ The blond he used to

first grand march they all would fall in line, Be - hind the man who
join them al - though ev' - ry thing was fine, But he stayed up - stairs and
waltz and glide with on the ball room floor, Is hap - py miss - is

was their joy and pride,_____ For _____
ex - er - cise his feet, _____ For _____
Ca - sey now for life, _____ For _____

CHORUS.
Valse

Ca - sey would waltz with a straw-ber - ry blonde, And the Band played

pay day came a - round each week they greased the floor with wax. And

Ca - sey was the fa - vor - ite and he that ran the ball. Of

thank'd them ver - y kind - ly for the fa vors they had shown. Then he'd

danced with noise and vig - or at the ball, _____ Each

kiss - ing and love - mak - ing did his share, _____ At

waltz once with the girl that he loved best. _____ Most

Sat - ur - day you'd see them dressed up in Sun - day clothes, Each

twelve o - clock ex - act - ly they all would fall in line, Then

all the friends are mar - ried that Ca - sey used to know, And

lad would have his sweet-heart by his side._____ When Ca - sey led the
march down to the din - ing hall and eat._____ But Ca - sey would not
Ca - sey too has tak - en him a wife._____ The blond he used to

first grand march they all would fall in line, Be - hind the man who
join them al - though ev' - ry thing was fine, But he stayed up - stairs and
waltz and glide with on the ball room floor, Is hap - py miss - is

was their joy and pride,_____ For _____
ex - er - cise his feet, _____ For _____
Ca - sey now for life, _____ For

CHORUS.
Valse

Ca - sey would waltz with a straw-ber - ry blonde, And the Band played

on, _____ He'd glide cross the floor with the girl he a - dor'd, and the Band

played on, _____ But his brain was so load-ed it near-ly ex-plod-ed, The

poor girl would shake with a - larm. _____ He'd ne'er leave the girl with the straw-ber-ry

curls, And the Band played on. _____

BELIEVE ME IF ALL THOSE ENDEARING YOUNG CHARMS,

Written by

Thomas Moore Esqr.

Arranged by

J. A. STEVENSON.

Philadelphia, George Willig 171 Chesnut Street

Voce.

Be_lieve me, if all those en_

dearing young charms, Which I gaze on so fond_ly to day, Were to change by to_mor_row and

fleet in my arms, Like fai_ry gifts fa_ding a_ _way Thou would'st

still be ador'd as this moment thou art, Let thy love_li_ness fade as it will; And a

round the dear ruin, each wish of my heart. Would en_twine it_self verdant_ly still.

It is not while beauty and youth are thine own,

And thy cheeks unprofan'd by a tear,

That the fervour and faith of a soul can be known,

To which time will but make thee more dear!

Oh! The heart, that has truly lov'd, never forgets,

But as truly loves on to the close;

As the sunflower turns on her God, when he sets,

COME BACK TO ERIN

SONG.

COMPOSED BY

CLARIBEL.

5

Copyrighted 1883

PUBLISHER
M. D. SWISHER
No. 123   S. 10th ST.
PHILADELPHIA

COME BACK TO ERIN.

Words and Music by

CLARIBEL.

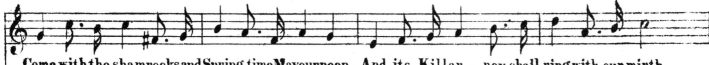

Come back to E - rin, Mavourneen, Mavourneen; Come back, A - roon, to the land of my birth:

O - ver the green sea, Mavourneen, Mavourneen, Long shone the white sail that bore thee a - way;

O may the an - gels, O wa - kin' and sleepin' Watch oe'r my bird in the land far a - way;

Come with the shamrocks and Spring-time Mavourneen, And its Killar - ney shall ring with our mirth.

Ri - ding the white waves that fair Summer morn-in', Just like a May-flow'r a float on the bay.

And it's my pray'rs will con-sign to their keep-in' Care o' my jew - el by night and by day.

Sure, when we lent ye to beau-ti-ful Eng-land,
O, but my heart sank when clouds came be-tween us,
When by the fire-side I watch the bright em-bers,

Lit-tle we thought of the lone win-ter days,
Like a grey cur-tain the rain fall-ing down,
Then all my heart flies to England and thee,

Lit-tle we thought of the hush of the star shine
Hid from my sad eyes the path o'er the o-cean
Cra-vin' to know if my dar-lin' remembers,

animato

O - ver the moun-tain, the bluffs and the brays! Then come back to E - rin, Ma-
Far, far a-way where my Col-leen had flown. Then come back to E - rin, Ma-
Or if her thoughts may be cross-in' to me. Then come back to E - rin, Ma-

Nº 1 in C   Nº 2 in D   Nº 3 in E♭   Nº 4 in F

SUNG BY

MME. SCHUMANN-HEINK, MISS FLORENCE HINKLE
AND
MR. DAN BEDDOE

DANNY BOY

Song

ADAPTED FROM AN

Old Irish Air

BY

FRED. E. WEATHERLY

Ⓐ

BOOSEY & COMPANY, INC.
NEW YORK: STEINWAY HALL, 113 WEST 57TH ST.
LONDON, ENG.: BOOSEY & CO., LTD., 295 REGENT ST., W.I.

DANNY BOY.

Words by
FRED. E. WEATHERLY.

Adapted from
an Old Irish Air by
FRED. E. WEATHERLY.

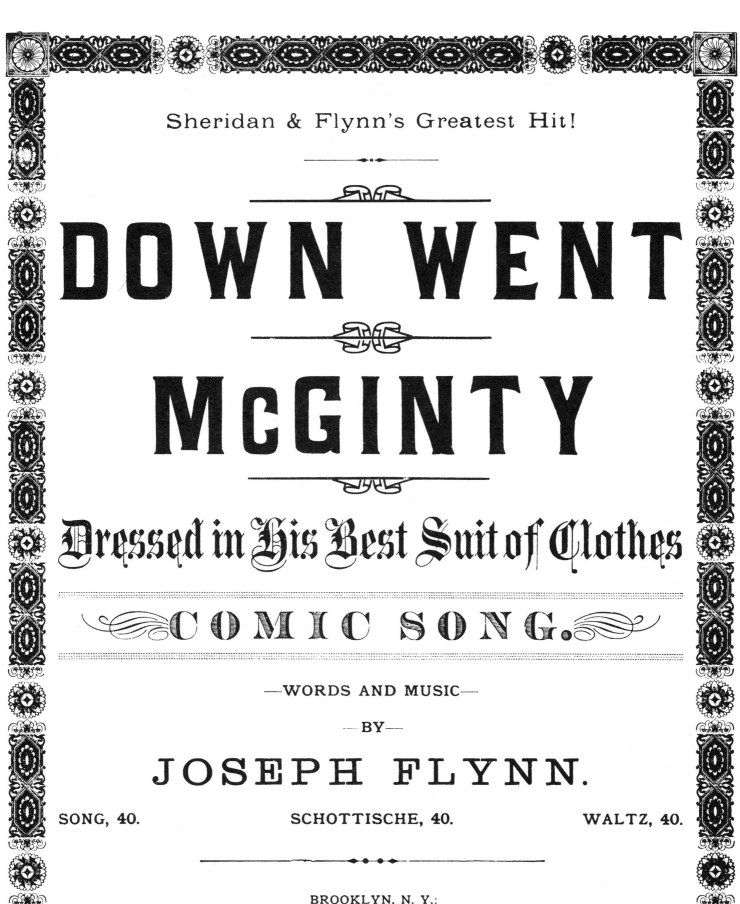

Sheridan & Flynn's Greatest Hit!

DOWN WENT McGINTY

Dressed in His Best Suit of Clothes

COMIC SONG.

—WORDS AND MUSIC—

—BY—

JOSEPH FLYNN.

SONG, 40. SCHOTTISCHE, 40. WALTZ, 40.

BROOKLYN, N. Y.:

PUBLISHED BY SPAULDING & KORNDER, 487 FULTON ST.

Down Went McGinty.

SONG AND CHORUS.

Words and Music by JOSEPH FLYNN.

1. Sun - day morn - ing just at nine, Dan Mc - Gin - ty dress'd so fine, Stood look-
2. From the hospi - tle Mac went home, When they fix'd his bro - ken bones, To find
3. Now Mc - Gin - ty raved and swore, About his clothes he felt so sore, And an
4. Now Mc - Gin - ty thin and pale One fine day got out of jail, And with

-ing up at a ver - y high stone wall; When his friend young Pat Mc-Cann, Says, I'll
he was the fa - ther of a child; So to cel - e - brate it right, His friends
oath he took he'd kill the man or die; So he tight - ly grabb'd his stick And hit
joy to see his boy was near - ly wild; To his house he quick - ly ran To meet

bet five dol - lars, Dan, | I could car - ry you to the top with - out a fall; ..... So on his
he went to in - vite, | And he soon was drink - ing whis - ky fast and wild; ..... Then he
the driv - er a lick, | Then he raised a lit - tle shan - ty on his eye; ..... But two po -
his wife Be - daley Ann, | But she'd skipp'd a - way and took a - long the child; ..... Then he

shoulders he took Dan To climb the ladder he began, And he soon commenc'd to reach up near the top; .... When Mc -
waddled down the street In his Sun-day suit so neat, Holding up his head as proud as John the Great, ... But in the
- lice-men saw the muss And they soon join'd in the fuss, Then they ran McGin-ty in for be - ing drunk; ... And the
gave up in despair, And he mad- ly pull'd his hair, As he stood one day up - on the riv - er shore, ... Know- ing

mf

Gin - ty, cute old rogue, To win the five he did let go, Nev- er think-ing just how far he'd have to drop. ....
side-walk was a hole, To re - ceive a ton of coal, That Mc- Gin - ty nev- er saw till just too late. ...
Judge says with a smile, We will keep you for a while In a cell to sleep up- on a pris - on bunk. ....
well he couldn't swim, He did fool - ish - ly jump in, Although wa - ter he had nev - er took be - fore. ...

CHORUS.

1st Cho. Down went McGin- ty to the bot- tom of the wall, And tho' he won the five, He was more dead than alive, Sure his
2d Cho. Down went McGin- ty to the bot- tom of the hole, Then the driv-er of the cart Give the load of coal a start, And it
3d Cho. Down went McGin- ty to the bot- tom of the jail Where his board would cost him nix, And he stay'd exact- ly six, They were
4th Cho. Down went McGin- ty to the bot- tom of the say, And he must be ver- y wet For they haven't found him yet, But they

ribs, and nose, and back were broke from getting such a fall, Dress'd in his best suit of clothes. . . .
took us half an hour to dig Mc- Gin- ty from the coal, Dress'd in his best suit of clothes. . . .
big long months he stopp'd For no one went his bail, Dress'd in his best suit of clothes. . . .
say his ghost comes round the docks Before the break of day, Dress'd in his best suit of clothes. . . .

IRISH COMIC SONG.

BY

THOMAS CASEY.

DRILL YE TARRIERS.

Sung by

MAGGIE CLINE.

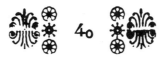

FOR SALE AT ALL MUSIC STORES.

NEW YORK:

FRANK HARDING'S MUSIC HOUSE.

Office, 1293 Broadway, Corner of 33d St.

C. H. DITSON & CO.
867 Broadway, N. Y.

OLIVER DITSON CO.
Boston, Mass.

LYON & HEALY.
Chicago, Ill.

Copies of our publications can be obtained or ordered of all Music sellers. Ask for the beautiful ballad by Graham, "Her Mem'ry Brings Me No Regret." Published for Pianoforte and Voice, Quartette, Orchestra and Cornet Solo.

"DRILL, YE TARRIERS, DRILL!"

As sung by

THOMAS CASEY.

1. Oh! ev-'ry morn' at seven o-'clock There are
2. The boss was a fine man all a-round But he
3. The new fore-man is Dan Mc Cann, I'll
4. When pay day next it came a-round, Poor

twen - ty   tar - riers on   the   rock, The   boss comes along and
mar - ried a great,   big, fat   far - down, She   baked good bread and
tell   you   sure he's a   blame mean man, Last   week   a   premature
Jim's   pay a dol - lar short he found, What   for? says he   then came

says "be   still And put all   your   power   in the cast - steel   drill."
baked it   well, And   baked   it   hard   as the hobs of   H—l.
blast went   off, And a   mile   in the air   went   big   Jim   Goff:
this   re - ply, "You were docked for the time   you were up   in the sky."

CHORUS.

Then   drill, ye   tar - riers, drill,   Drill, ye   tar - riers,

drill. Oh it's work all day without sug-ar in your tay when ye work be - yant on the rail - way, And drill, ye tar - riers drill. drill. (Spoken.)

*Spoken, 1st Verse. Stand out there with the flag, Sullivan. Stand back there! Blast! Fire! All over!

" 2d " Stand out forninst the fence with the flag, McCarthy. Stand back, etc.

" 3d " Where's the fuse. McGinty? What, he lit his pipe with it! Stop the Belt car coming down. Stand back, etc.

" 4th " More oatmeal in the bucket, McCue. What's that your reading, Duffy, the Staats Zeitung? Get out there with the flag, etc.

The Harp that once through Tara's Halls.

Written by

T. MOORE ESQ.ͬ

The Symphonies and Accompaniments

By

SIR JOHN STEVENSON.

Published by John Cole Baltimore.

The Harp that once, thro' Tara's halls, The soul of music shed, Now hangs as mute on

Tara's walls As if that soul were fled; So sleeps the pride of former days, So glo _ ry's thrill is o'er And hearts that once beat high for praise, Now feel that pulse no more!.

2

No more to chiefs and ladies bright

    The harp of Tara swells;

The chord, alone, that breaks at night,

    Its tale of ruin tells.

Thus freedom now so seldom wakes,

    The only throb she gives,

Is when some heart indignant breaks,

    To shew that still she lives!

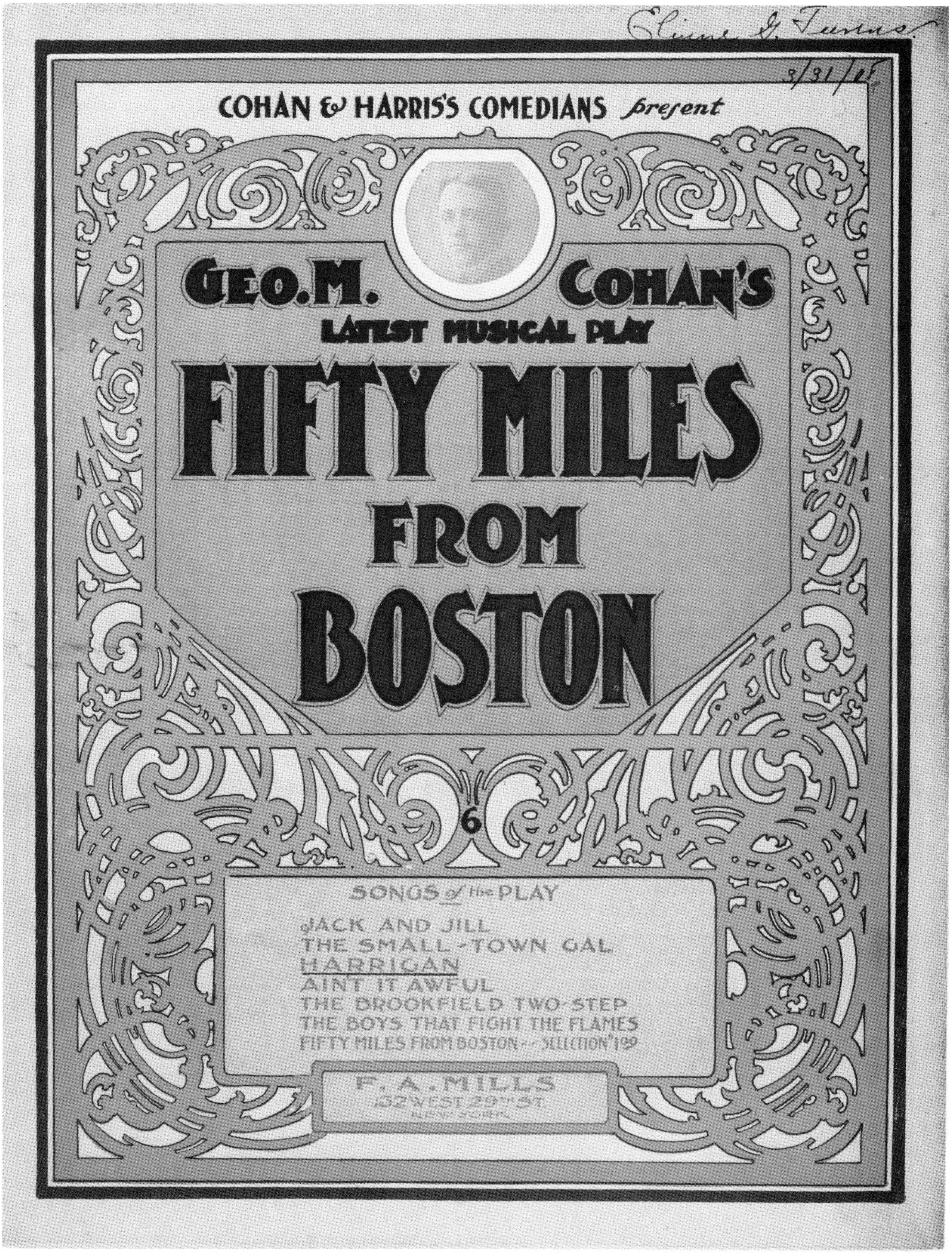
Eliine G. Turns.
3/31/05
COHAN & HARRIS'S COMEDIANS present
GEO. M. COHAN'S
LATEST MUSICAL PLAY
FIFTY MILES FROM BOSTON
6
SONGS of the PLAY
JACK AND JILL
THE SMALL-TOWN GAL
HARRIGAN
AIN'T IT AWFUL
THE BROOKFIELD TWO-STEP
THE BOYS THAT FIGHT THE FLAMES
FIFTY MILES FROM BOSTON -- SELECTION $1.00
F. A. MILLS
32 WEST 29TH ST.
NEW YORK

"Harrigan."

GEO. M. COHAN.

Moderato.

SOLO.

Who   is   the man   who will   spend   or   will   ev - en   lend?
Who   is   the man   nev - er   stood   for   a   gad   a - bout?

till ready

CHORUS.   SOLO.

Har - ri - gan,   That's me! —   Who   is   your friend when   you
Har - ri - gan,   That's me! —   Who   is   the man   that the

CHORUS.   SOLO.

find   that   you   need   a   friend?   Har - ri - gan,   That's me! —   For
town's sim - ply   mad   a - bout?   Har - ri - gan,   That's me! —   The

28

I'm just as proud of my name you see, As an Em-per-or, Czar or a
la-dies and ba-bies are fond of me, I'm fond of them, too, in re-

King, could be: Who is the man helps a
turn, you see: Who is the gent helps that's de-

CHORUS. SOLO.

man ev-'ry time he can? Har-ri-gan, That's me!__
ser-ving a mon-u-ment? Har-ri-gan, That's me!__

CHORUS.

H - A - dou-ble R - I - G - A - N spells Har-ri-gan,

Proud of all the I-rish blood that's in me; Div-il a man can say a word a-

gin me. H - A - dou - ble R - I -

G - A - N, you see,＿＿＿＿＿ Is a name that a shame nev-er

has been con-nect-ed with. Har-ri-gan, That's me!＿ me.＿

HAS ANYBODY HERE SEEN KELLY?

WRITTEN & COMPOSED
BY
C.W.MURPHY
&
WILL·LETTERS

SUCCESSFULLY·INTRODUCED
BY
NORA·BAYES
OF
BAYES·&·NORWORTH
IN
LEW·FIELDS
PRODUCTION
THE·JOLLY·BACHELORS

T·B·HARMS·&·FRANCIS·DAY·&·HUNTER·NEW·YORK   6

GENE
BUCK

Has Anybody Here Seen Kelly!

American Version by
William J. Mc Kenna.

Written & Composed by
C. W. Murphy & Will Letters.

Mich-ael Kel-ly with his sweet-heart came from Coun-ty Cork, And
Ov-er on fifth Av-en-ue, a band be-gan to play, Ten

bent up-on a hol-i-day, they land-ed in New-York. They
thou-sand men were march-ing for it was Saint Pat-rick's day. The

strolled a-round to see the sights a-las, it's sad to say, Poor
"Wear-ing of the Green" rang out up-on the morn-ing air, 'Twas

Kel - ly lost his lit - tle girl up - on the Great White Way, She
Kel - ly's fav - 'rite song, so Ma - ry said, "I'll find him there." She

walked up - town from Her - ald Square to for - ty sec - ond street the
climbed up - on the grand stand in___ hopes her Mike she'd see, 'Five

traf - fic stopped as, she cried to the cop - per on the beat.
hun - dred Kel - ly's left the ranks in an - swer to her plea.

Chorus.

Has an - y - bod - y here seen Kel - ly?___ K. E.

Has Anybody Here Seen Kelly?   33

I'LL TAKE YOU HOME AGAIN,

KATHLEEN.

SONG AND CHORUS.

WORDS AND MUSIC BY

THOMAS P. WESTENDORF.

CINCINNATI.

Published by JOHN CHURCH & CO. 66 W. Fourth St.

CHICAGO.   NEW YORK.

Root & Sons Music Co.   J. Church & Co.

I'll Take You Home Again, Kathleen.

Words and Music by THOMAS P. WESTENDORF.

1. I'll take you home a-gain, Kath-leen, A - cross the o - cean wild and
2. I know you love me, Kath-leen, dear, Your heart was ev - er fond and
3. To that dear home be-yond the sea, My Kath - leen shall a - gain re-

wide, To where your heart has ev - er been, Since
true; I al - ways feel when you are near, That
turn, And when thy old friends wel-come thee, Thy

first you were my bon - ny bride.   The ro - - ses all have left your
life holds noth - ing dear but you.   The smiles that once you gave to
lov - - ing heart will cease to yearn.   Where laughs the lit - tle sil - ver

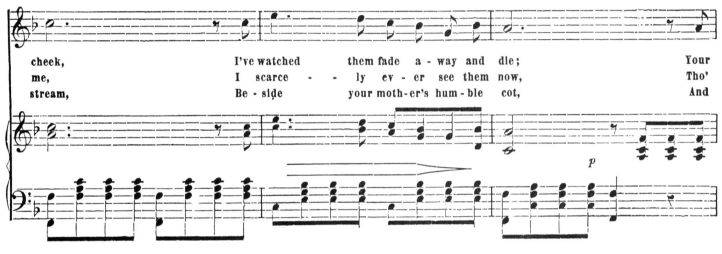

cheek,   I've watched them fade a - way and die;   Your
me,   I scarce - - ly ev - er see them now,   Tho'
stream,   Be - side your moth - er's hum - ble cot,   And

voice is sad when e'er you speak,   And tears be - dim your lov - ing eyes.
ma - ny, ma - ny times I see   A dark - - 'ning sha - dow on your brow.
bright - est rays of sun - shine gleam, There all your grief will be for - got.

CHORUS.

I'VE GOT RINGS ON MY FINGERS

OR · MUMBO · JUMBO · JIJJIBOO · J. O'SHAY

BLANCHE RING'S

GREATEST SUCCESS

AS INTRODUCED IN

THE YANKEE GIRL

Words by
WESTON & BARNES

Music by
MAURICE SCOTT

T. B. HARMS & FRANCIS, DAY & HUNTER
NEW YORK

"I've Got Rings On My Fingers;"

or, Mumbo Jumbo Jijjiboo J. O'Shea.

Words by
Weston and Barnes.

Music by
Maurice Scott.

1. Jim O-'Shea was cast a-way Up-on an In-dian isle, The
2. O'er the sea went Rose Mc Gee To see her na-bob grand, He
3. Em-'rald green he robed his queen, To share with him his throne, 'Mid

na-tives there they lik'd his hair, They lik'd his I-rish smile, So
sat with-in his pal-an-quin, And when she'd kissed his hand, He
eas-tern charms and wav-ing palms, They'd sham-rocks, I-rish grown, Sent

KATHLEEN MAVOURNEEN

SONG
COMPOSED BY

F. N. CROUCH.

BOSTON.

Published by OLIVER DITSON & CO. 451 Washington St.

KATHLEEN MAVOURNEEN.

Composed by F. W. N. CROUCH.

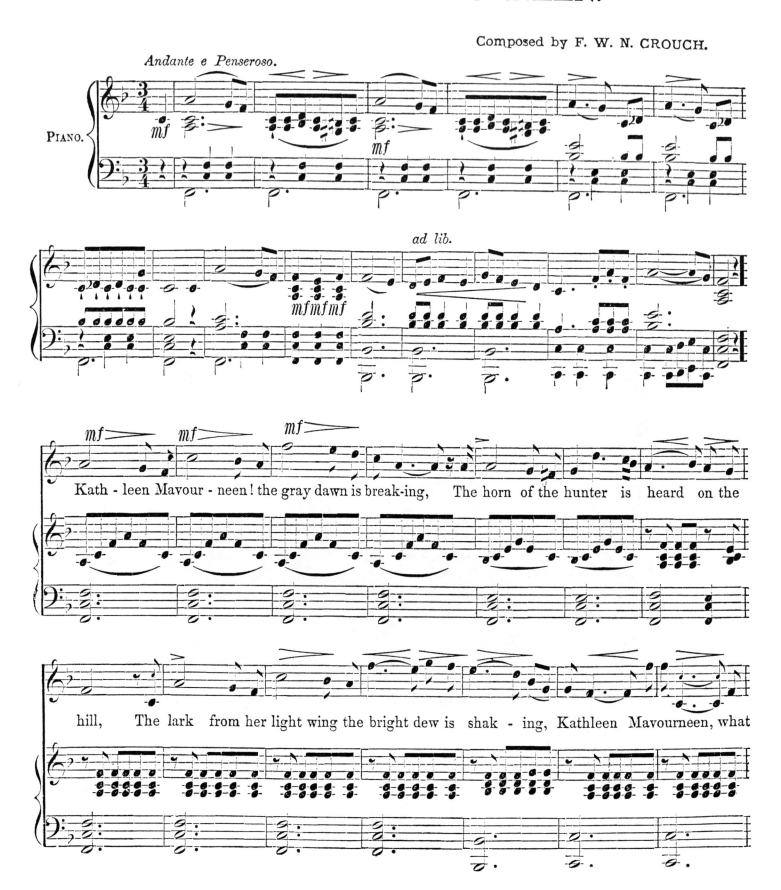

44

slum - ber-ing still? Oh! hast thou for-gotten how soon we must sever? Oh! hast thou for-gotten this day we must part, It may be for years, and it may be for-ever, Oh! why art thou silent thou voice of my heart? It may be for years, and it may be for - ever, Then why art thou silent Kathleen Ma-

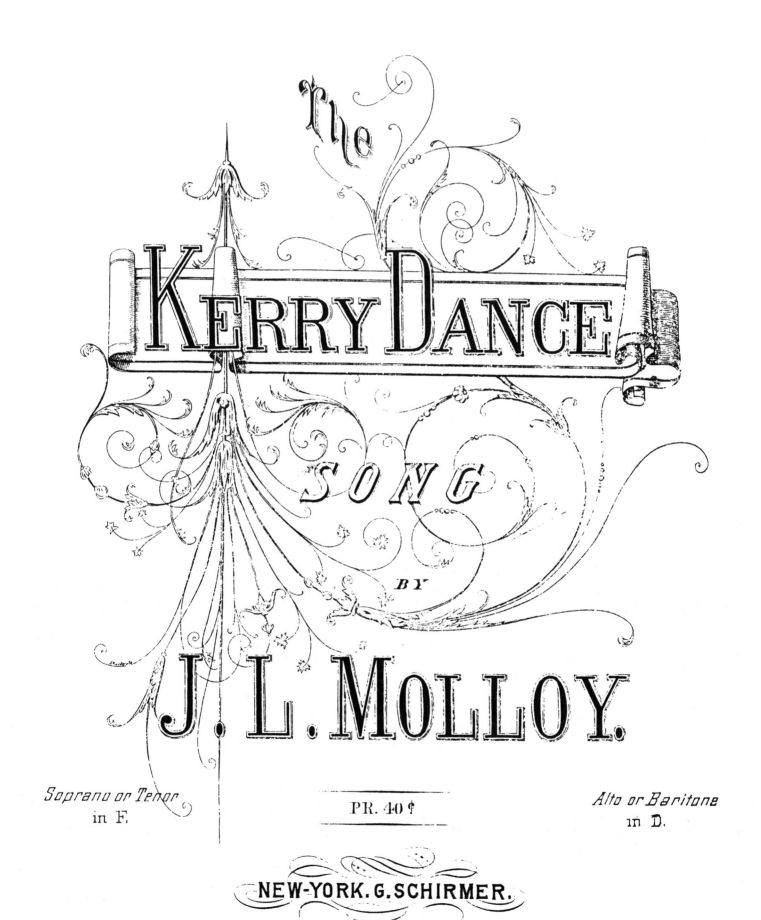

The Kerry Dance

Song

by

J. L. Molloy.

Soprano or Tenor
in F.

PR. 40 ¢

Alto or Baritone
in D.

NEW-YORK. G. SCHIRMER.

THE KERRY DANCE.

Words and Music
by **J. L. MOLLOY.**

49

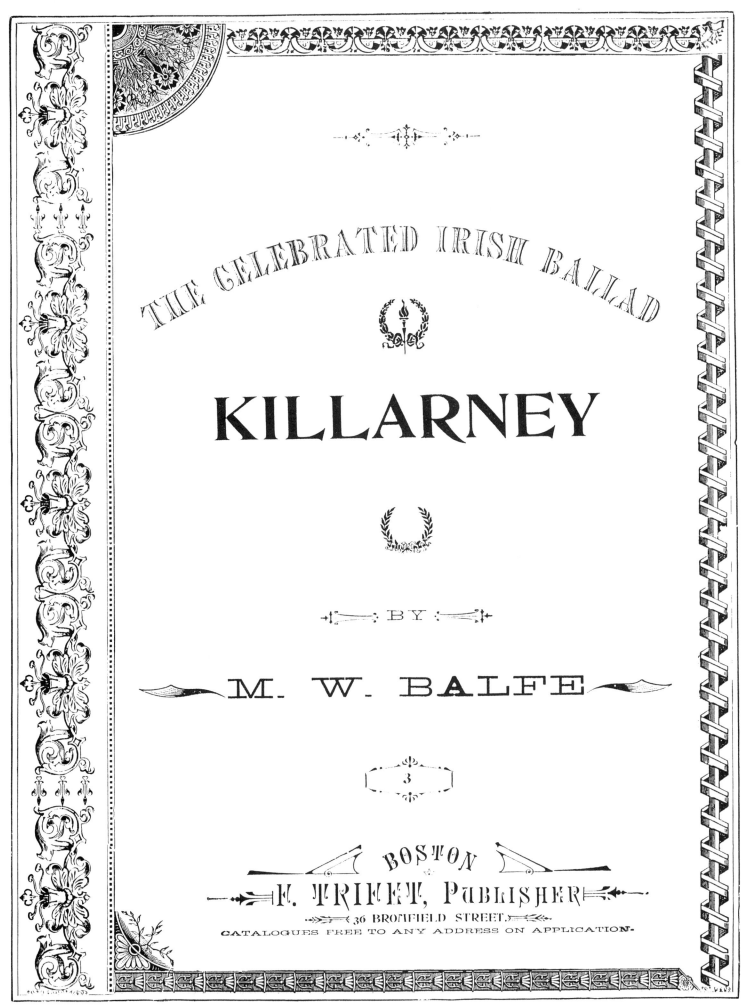

THE CELEBRATED IRISH BALLAD

KILLARNEY

BY

M. W. BALFE

3

BOSTON

F. TRIFET, Publisher

36 BROMFIELD STREET.

CATALOGUES FREE TO ANY ADDRESS ON APPLICATION.

KILLARNEY.

M. W. BALFE.

56

loves all lands, Beau-ty wan-ders ev'-ry-where, Footprints leaves on ma-ny strands,—
Gle-na bay: Moun-tains Tore and Ea-gles' Nest, Still at Mucross you must pray,
green grass grows, Ev'-ry morn springs na-tal day, Bright-hued ber-ries daff the snows,
tints be-low, Seems the heav'n a-bove to vie: All rich col-ors that we know,

rall. 3 *dim.* *pp* *a tempo.*

But her home is sure-ly there; An-gels fold their wings and rest In that E-den
Tho' the monks are now at rest; An-gels won-der not that man There would fain pro-
Smil-ing win-ter's frown a-way. An-gels, oft-ten paus-ing there, Doubt if E-den
Tinge the cloud-wreath in that sky. Wings of an-gels so might shine, Glanc-ing back soft

colla parte. *rit.* *pp* *a tempo.*

cres. *f*

of the west, Beau-ty's home, Kil-lar - - ney, Ev-er fair Kil-lar-ney.
long life's span, Beau-ty's home, Kil-lar - - ney, Ev-er fair Kil-lar-ney.
were more fair, Beau-ty's home, Kil-lar - - ney, Ev-er fair Kil-lar-ney.
light di-vine, Beau-ty's home, Kil-lar - - ney, Ev-er fair Kil-lar-ney.

THE LATEST CRAZE.

LITTLE
ANNIE ROONEY.

SONG AND CHORUS.

WRITTEN, COMPOSED AND SUNG BY

MICHAEL NOLAN.

→ 40 ←

NEW YORK:
HITCHCOCK'S MUSIC STORES,
385 SIXTH AVENUE,
11 PARK ROW,   283 SIXTH AVENUE,
294 GRAND STREET.

Chicago, Ill.: NATIONAL MUSIC CO., 215 Wabash Avenue.

LITTLE ANNIE ROONEY.

Written, Composed and Sung by MICHAEL NOLAN.

1. A win-ning way, a pleas-ant smile, Dress'd so neat but quite in style,
2. The par-lor's small, but neat and clean, And set with taste so sel-dom seen, And
3. We've been en-gaged close on a year, The hap-py time is draw-ing near, I'll

Mer-ry chaff your time to wile, Has lit-tle An-nie Roon---ey.
you can bet, the house-hold queen, Is lit-tle An-nie Roon---ey. The
wed the one I love so dear, Lit-tle An-nie Roon---ey. My

59

Ev' - ry eve - ning, rain or shine, I make a call twixt eight and nine, On
fire burns cheer - ful - ly and bright, As a fami - ly cir - cle round each night, We
friends de - clare I'm in a jest, Un - til the time comes will not rest, But

her who short - ly will be mine,.... Lit - tle An - nie Roon - - - ey.
form, and ev' - ry one's de - light Is lit - tle An - nie Roon - - - ey.
one who knows its val - ue best, Is lit - tle An - nie Roon - - - ey.

CHORUS.
p, 2nd time, ff

She's my sweet - heart, I'm her beau ;........ She's

my An - nie,...... I'm her Joe,......... Soon we'll

In F

In Ab

In Bb

In C

SUNG BY

MR. CHAUNCEY OLCOTT

IN

THE HEART OF PADDY WHACK

A LITTLE BIT OF HEAVEN SHURE THEY CALL IT IRELAND

(HOW IRELAND GOT IT'S NAME)

SONG

LYRIC BY

J. KEIRN BRENNAN

MUSIC BY

ERNEST R. BALL

Composer of "MOTHER MACHREE", "WHO KNOWS?", "MY DEAR",
"WHEN IRISH EYES ARE SMILING", "IN THE GARDEN OF MY HEART,"
"TILL THE SANDS OF THE DESERT GROW COLD", "IRISH EYES OF LOVE" *etc.*

Price 60 cents.

M. WITMARK & SONS,

NEW YORK • CHICAGO • LONDON.

A Little Bit Of Heaven

Shure They Call It Ireland

Have you ever heard the story of how Ireland got its name?
I'll tell you so you'll understand from whence old Ireland came;
No wonder that we're proud of that dear land across the sea,
For here's the way me dear old mother told the tale to me:

Shure, a little bit of Heaven fell from out the sky one day,
And nestled on the ocean in a spot so far away;
And when the angels found it, shure it looked so sweet and fair,
They said,"Suppose we leave it, for it looks so peaceful there:"
So they sprinkled it with star dust just to make the shamrocks grow,
'Tis the only place you'll find them, no matter where you go;
Then they dotted it with silver, to make its lakes so grand,
And when they had it finished, shure they called it Ireland.

'Tis a dear old land of fairies and of wond'rous wishing wells,
And no where else on God's green earth have they such lakes and dells!
No wonder that the angels loved its Shamrock-bordered shore,
'Tis a little bit of Heaven, and I love it more and more.

J. Keirn Brennan

Dedicated to Rita Olcott

A Little Bit Of Heaven
Shure They Call It Ireland

Poem by
J. KEIRN BRENNAN

Music by
ERNEST R. BALL

Moderately, with expression

Have you ev-er heard the sto-ry of how Ire-land got its name? I'll
'Tis a dear old land of fair-ies and of won-drous wish-ing wells; And

tell you so you'll un-der-stand from whence old Ire-land came.___ No
no where else on God's green earth have they such lakes and dells.___ No

won-der that we're proud of that dear land a-cross the sea,___ For
won-der that the An-gels loved its Sham-rock bor-dered shore,___ 'Tis a

64

here's the way me dear old moth-er told the tale to me.__
lit-tle bit of Heav-en, and I love it more and more.__

Shure, a lit-tle bit of Heav-en fell from out the sky one day,__ And

nes-tled on the o-cean in a spot so far a-way;__ And

when the An-gels found it, Shure it looked so sweet and fair,__ They

said, Sup-pose we leave it, for it looks so peace-ful there! So they

sprink-led it with star dust just to make the sham-rocks grow;— 'Tis the

on-ly place you'll find them, no mat-ter where you go;— Then they dot-ted it with sil-ver To

make its lakes so grand, And when they had it fin-ished shure they called it Ire-land.—

No. 1 in F

No. 2 in A♭

No. 3 in B♭

SUNG BY
MR JOHN MCCORMACK
AND BY
MR CHAUNCEY OLCOTT
IN HIS NEW PLAY "MACUSHLA"

MACUSHLA

THE WORDS BY

JOSEPHINE V. ROWE

The Music by

DERMOT MACMURROUGH.

PRICE 60 CENTS

BOOSEY & CO
9 EAST SEVENTEENTH STREET, NEW YORK
AND
295 REGENT STREET, LONDON, ENG.

MACUSHLA

Words by
JOSEPHINE V. ROWE

Music by
DERMOT MACMURROUGH

(Minstrel Boy. 3.)

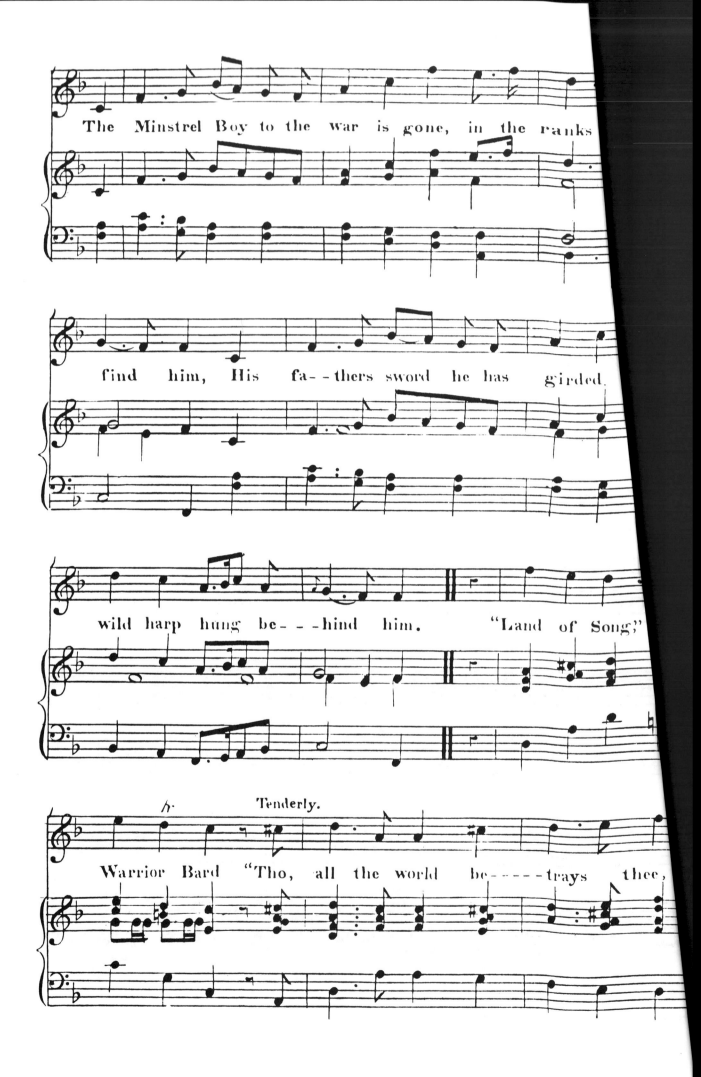

The Minstrel Boy to the war is gone, in the ranks

find him, His fa- -thers sword he has girded.

wild harp hung be- - -hind him. "Land of Song,"

Warrior Bard "Tho, all the world be- - - - - -trays thee,

Tenderly.

sword at least thy Right shall guard, One faith--ful Harp shall

praise thee.

2

The Minstrel fell! but the foeman's chain

Could not bring his proud soul under;

The Harp he lov'd ne'er spoke again,

For he tore its Chords asunder;

And said "No chains shall sully thee,

Thou soul of Love and Bravery!

"Thy songs were made for the pure and free,

"They shall never sound in Slavery."

MOLLY BAWN

IRISH BALLAD,

Sung by

M. BALFE,

in the Comic Operetta of

Il Paddy Whack in Italia.

Written & Composed by

SAMUEL LOVER ESQ.

NEW YORK, Published by Wm. DUBOIS 285 Broadway.

PHILADELPHIA, A. FIOT 196 Chesnut street.

ANDANTE NON TROPPO E GRAZIOSO.

Now the pret-ty flow'rs were made to bloom dear, And the pret-ty stars were made to shine; And the pret--ty girls were made for the boys dear, And may be you were made for mine. The wick--ed watch-dog here is snarling, He takes me for a thief you see, For he knows I'd steal you Molly

FAVORITE SONGS

MOLLY MALONE. High (B♭), Medium (G).
Old Irish Melody . . . . Arr. by W. Rhys-Herbert .50

GO WHERE GLORY WAITS THEE. High (E♭).
Low (D♭).
Air: Maid of the Valley. Arr. by W. Rhys-Herbert .50

ANNIE O' THE MOY. High (A♭) . . . . J. Wiegand .40

THIS DEAR LITTLE SHAMROCK. Song and
Chorus . . . . W. A. Ogden .40

A HANDFUL OF EARTH. Song and Chorus. W. H. Clark .30

Published by

J. FISCHER & BRO.
NEW YORK

MBLFETE

Molly Malone.

MEDIUM.

OLD IRISH MELODY.
Arr. by W. RHYS-HERBERT.

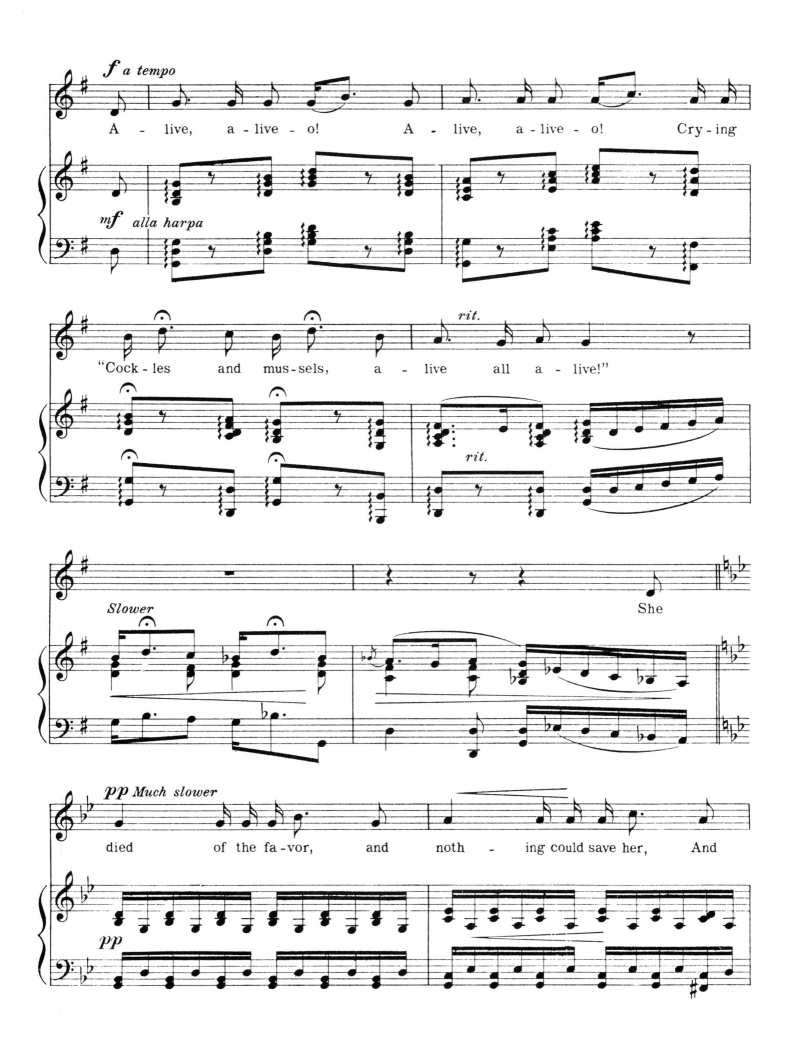

SUNG BY
CHAUNCEY OLCOTT
AND
JOHN MᶜCORMACK.

Duet
Two Keys

In B♭

Contralto or
Baritone
(Lead)
and
Soprano or
Tenor

In F

Soprano or
Tenor
(Lead)
and
Contralto or
Baritone

MOTHER MACHREE

··· Song ···

LYRIC BY

RIDA JOHNSON YOUNG

MUSIC BY

CHAUNCEY OLCOTT AND ERNEST R. BALL

Solo 60 Cents

Duet 75 Cents

M. WITMARK & SONS,

NEW YORK · CHICAGO · SAN FRANCISCO · LONDON · PARIS.

Mother Machree.

Lyric by
RIDA JOHNSON YOUNG.

Music by
CHAUNCEY OLCOTT
& ERNEST R. BALL.

Allegretto, ma espressivo.

There's a spot in me heart which no col-leen may own, There's a
Ev-'ry sor-row or care in the dear days gone by, Was made

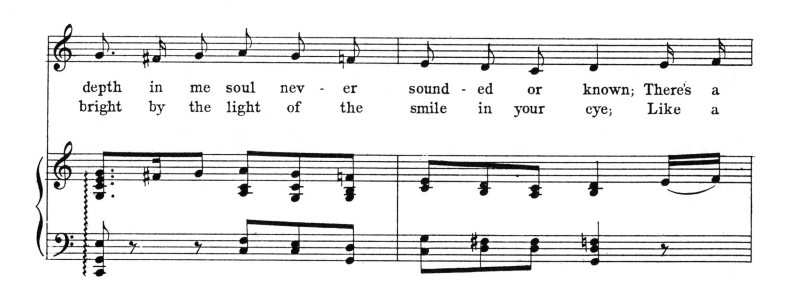

depth in me soul nev-er sound-ed or known; There's a
bright by the light of the smile in your eye; Like a

place in my mem - 'ry, my life, that you fill, No
can - dle that's set in a win - dow at night, No

molto rall.

oth - er can take it, no one ev - er will.
fond love has cheered me, and guid - ed me right.

molto rall.

Tenderly with much expression

Sure, I love the dear sil - ver that shines in your hair, And the

mp espress.

To MR. JOSH. HART.

THE

MULLIGAN GUARD

Composed, arranged & performed with immense success by

HARRIGAN & HART.

NEW YORK,

Published by Wm. A. Pond & Co. 547 Broadway.

QUICKSTEP.

SONG.

CHICAGO,   SAN FRANCISCO,   ST. PAUL,   PITTSBURG,   MILWAUKEE,   SAVANNAH,   SAN JOSE,   HOUSTON,   NEW HAVEN.
ROOT & LEWIS.   M. GRAY.   WEIDE & ROSS.   H. KLEBER & BRO.   H. N. HEMPSTED.   LUDDEN & BATES.   A. WALDTEUFEL.   E. H. CUSHING.   SKINNER & SPERRY

ENT'D ACCORDING TO ACT OF CONGRESS IN THE YEAR 1873 BY Wm A. POND & Co. IN THE OFFICE OF LIBRARIAN OF CONGRESS AT WASHINGTON. D. C.

THE MULLIGAN GUARD.

Composed and arranged by DAVID BRAHAM.

We crave your con-de-scension, We'll tell you what we know Of marching in the Mulligan Guard from Sli-go ward below. Our

Entered according to Act of Congress, A. D. 1873, by Wm. A. POND & CO. in the Office of the Librarian of Congress, at Washington.

90

Captain's name was Hussey, a Tipper - ra - ry man, He carried his sword like a Russian duke, when-

-ever he took com - mand. We shoulder'd guns, and march'd, and march'd a - way, From

FORWARD MARCH.

Bax - ter street, we march'd to Avenue A, With drums and fife, how sweet - ly they did

1st.

2d.

play, As we march'd, march'd, march'd in the Mulligan Guard. We Guard........

Dal Segno.

After the Second Verse.

2
When the band play'd Garry Owen,
Or the Connamara Pet;
With a rub a dub, dub, we'd march
In the mud, to the military step.
With the green above the red, boys,
To show where we come from,
Our guns we'd lift with the right shoulder shift,
As we'd march to the bate of the drum.—CHORUS.

3
Whin we got home at night, boys,
The divil a bite we'd ate,
We'd all set up and drink a sup
Of whiskey strong and nate.
Thin we'd all march home together,
As slippery as lard,
The solid min would all fall in,
And march with the Mulligan Guard.—CHORUS.

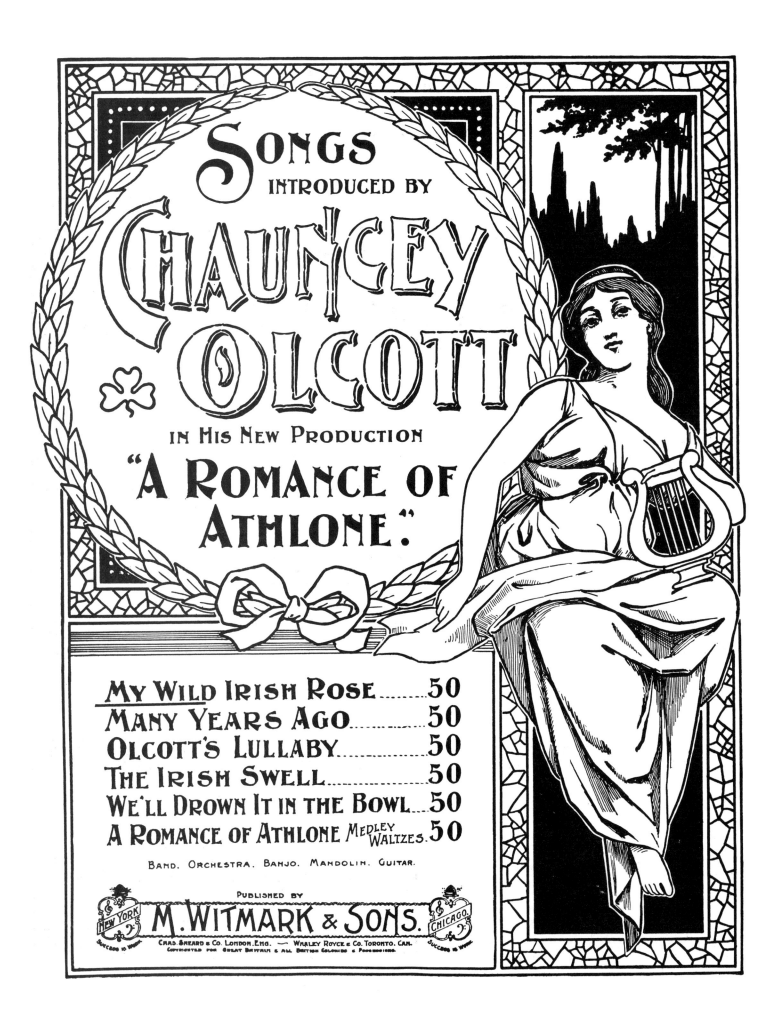

SONGS
INTRODUCED BY
CHAUNCEY
OLCOTT
IN HIS NEW PRODUCTION
"A ROMANCE OF
ATHLONE."

BAND. ORCHESTRA. BANJO. MANDOLIN. GUITAR.

PUBLISHED BY
NEW YORK M. WITMARK & SONS. CHICAGO
CHAS. SHEARD & CO. LONDON, ENG. — WHALEY ROYCE & CO. TORONTO, CAN.
COPYRIGHTED FOR GREAT BRITAIN & ALL BRITISH COLONIES & POSSESSIONS.

MY WILD IRISH ROSE.

Words and Music by CHAUNCEY OLCOTT.

Moderato.

mf

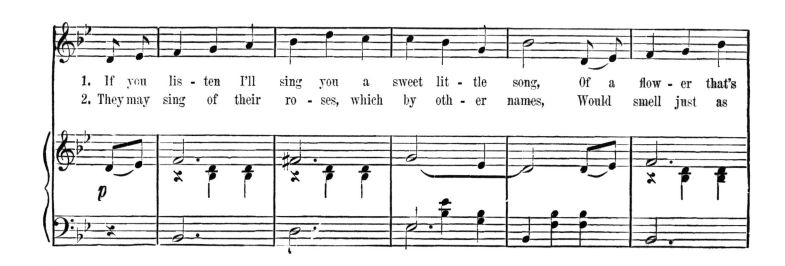

1. If you lis - ten I'll sing you a sweet lit - tle song, Of a flow - er that's
2. They may sing of their ro - ses, which by oth - er names, Would smell just as

p

now droped and dead........ Yet dear - er to me, yes, than all of its mates, Tho'
sweet - ly, they say........ But I know that my Rose, would nev - er con - sent, To have

each holds a - loft its proud head......... 'Twas giv - en to me by a girl that I
that sweet name tak - en a - way........ Her glan - ces are shy when e'er I pass

know, Since we've met, faith I've known no re - pose,......... She is dear - er by
by, The bow - er where my true love grows,........ And my one wish has

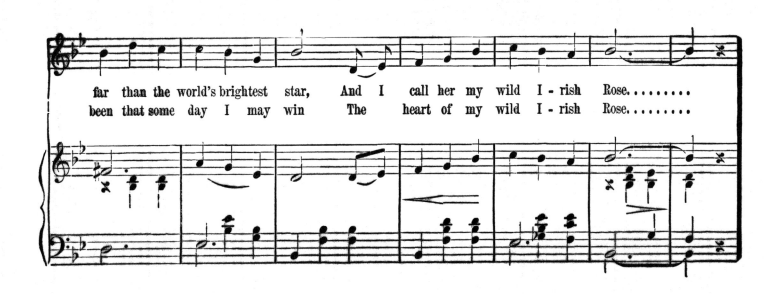

far than the world's brightest star, And I call her my wild I - rish Rose.........
been that some day I may win The heart of my wild I - rish Rose.........

CHORUS.

My wild I - rish Rose,........ the sweet-est flow'r that grows....... You may search ev - 'ry-where, but none can com - pare, With my wild I - rish Rose......... My wild I - rish Rose,........ The dear - est flow'r that grows,...... And some day for my sake, she may let me take, The bloom from my wild I - rish Rose........

OFT IN THE STILLY NIGHT

WRITTEN BY

THOMAS MOORE ESQ.

ARRANGED FOR THE

PIANO FORTE

BY

SIR JOHN STEVENSON.

New York WM. HALL & SON, 239 Broadway.

With melancholy expression.

Oft in the stil - - ly night, Ere slum-ber's chain has bound me, Fond mem'ry brings the light of o - ther days a - round me; The smiles the tears of boy hood's years, The

words of love then spo - ken, The eyes that shone, now dimm'd and gone, The cheer-ful hearts now

bro - ken! Thus in the stilly night, Ere slumber's chain has bound me, Sad mem'ry

brings the light of other days a - round me.

2

When I remember all
 The friends so linked together,
I've seen around me fall
 Like leaves in wintry weather;
I feel like one who treads alone
 Some banquet hall deserted,
Whose lights are fled, whose garlands dead,
 And all but he departed!
Thus in the stilly night,
 Ere slumbers chain hath bound me,
Sad mem'ry brings the light
 Of other days around me,

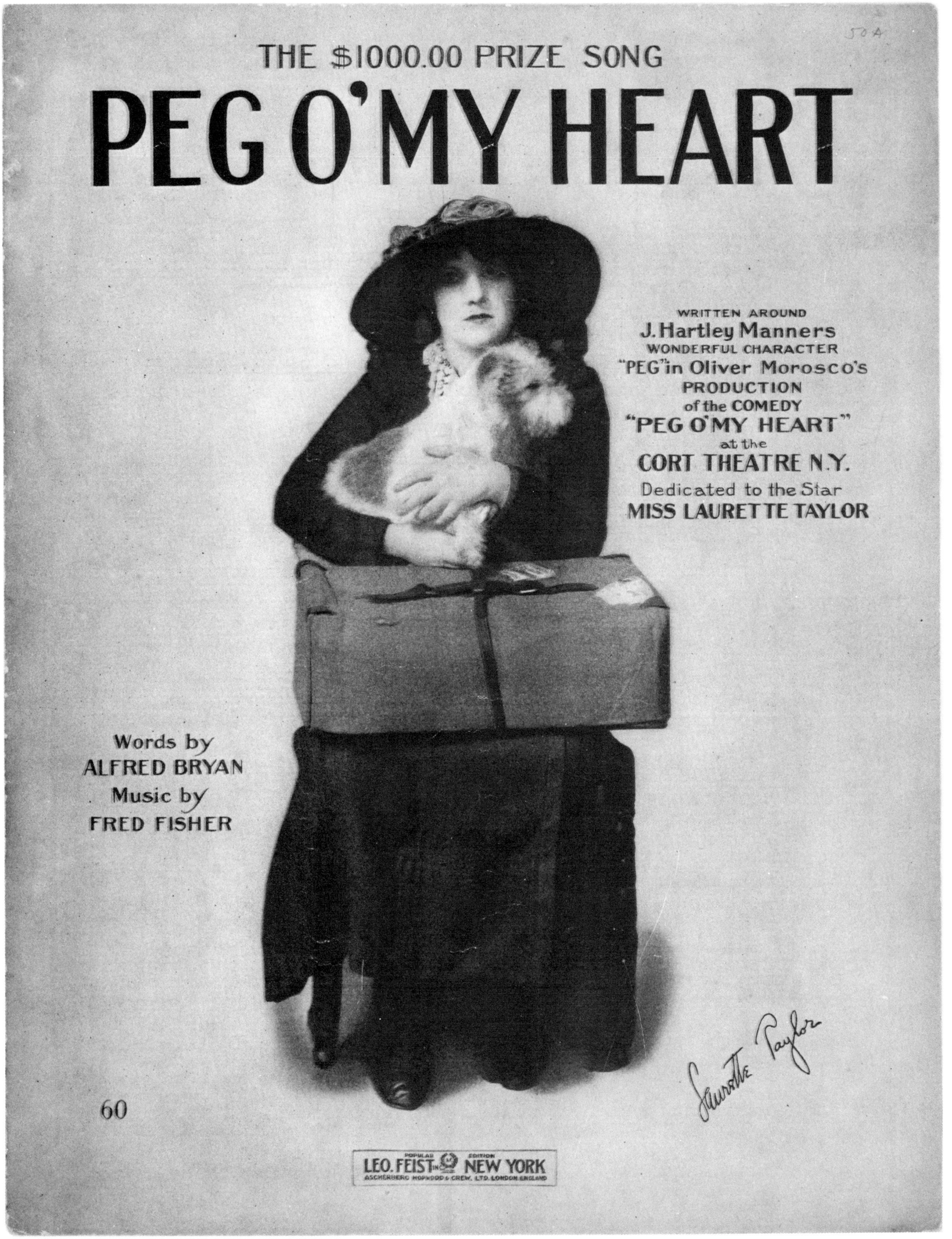

THE $1000.00 PRIZE SONG

PEG O' MY HEART

WRITTEN AROUND
J. Hartley Manners
WONDERFUL CHARACTER
"PEG" in Oliver Morosco's
PRODUCTION
of the COMEDY
"PEG O' MY HEART"
at the
CORT THEATRE N.Y.
Dedicated to the Star
MISS LAURETTE TAYLOR

Words by
ALFRED BRYAN
Music by
FRED FISHER

60

LEO. FEIST INC. NEW YORK
POPULAR EDITION
ASCHERBERG HOPWOOD & CREW. LTD. LONDON ENGLAND

99

Peg O' My Heart.

Words by
ALFRED BRYAN

Music by
FRED. FISCHER

Oh! my heart's in a whirl, Ov - er
When your heartsfull of fears, And your

one lit - tle girl, I love her, I love her, yes, I
eyes full of tears, I'll kiss them, I'll kiss them all a -

Sweet-er than the rose of Er-in, are your win-ning smiles en-dear-in', Peg O' My Heart,

Your glan-ces with Ir-ish art en-trance us,

Come, be my own,— Come, make your home in my heart.

heart.

COLLEEN DHAS CRUTHEN NA MOE,

The pretty Girl milking her Cow,

AN ANCIENT IRISH MELODY,

The Poetry Translated from the Original Irish

SUNG BY

Mrs. Waylett

with enthusiastic applause at the

LONDON AND DUBLIN THEATRES,

Arranged with

Symphonies & Accompaniments

BY

Alexander Lee.

This being Copyright can only be Sold at full Price.

Ent. Sta. Hall.

Pr. 2

LONDON

Published by Geo Shade Soho Square & H.L. Shade, Parliament St. Dublin.

of whom may be had Composed by A. Lee

MY LOVE SAILS O'ER THE BLUE WATERS.	FARE THEE WELL! OVER THE WATERS.
CHIME OUT SWEET BELLS.	SWEET IS THE TWILIGT HOUR.
DAUGHTERS OF MY SUNNY ITALY.	OH BLAME NOT MY LYRE.
THOU WILT GO & FORGET ME.	'TIS LOVE'S HALLOWED HOUR.
WHEN THE DEW IS ON THE GRASS.	THE BOY OF THE MOUNTAIN.
D.º FOR THE GUITAR.	WHEN THY CHARMS ARE ALL WITHER'D.

The World has won me fra thee Willie	C.B. Wilson.	
Water Drinker 2.ⁿᵈ Edit.ⁿ	Aaron Fry.	
Merry Spring	H. Russell.	
Sun has Set		E. Rogers.
Ask me Why		Crouch.
She is Fair as the Lily		Seymour.

COLLEEN DHAS CRUTHEN NA MOE,

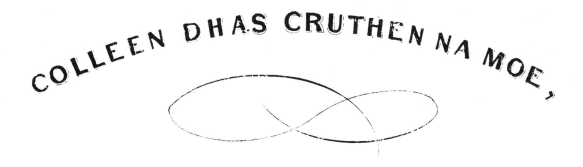

Composed by Alexander Lee.

Colleen dhas crutha na moe.

2.ᵈ VERSE.

Then to her I made my ad - van - - ces; "Good morrow, most beauti - ful

maid! Your beauty my heart so en....tran........ces", "Pray

Sir, do not banter," she said........"I'm not such a rare precious Jewel, That

I should enamour you so, I am but a poor little milk girl" Says

Colleen dhas crutheen na moe.

3d. VERSE.

The Indies afford no such Jew-----el So bright and transpa-rently

clear, Ah! do not add flame to my fu-el!— Con---------

THE ROSE OF TRALEE

Words by

E. Mordaunt Spencer

MUSIC BY

CHARLES W. GLOVER.

BOSTON Published by C.BRADLEE & C°. 194 Washington St.

The pale moon was ri - sing a - bove the green mountain, The

sun was de - clin - ing be - neath the blue sea, When I

stray'd with my love to the pure crystal fountain That stands in the beau-tiful

vale of Tra-lee: She was lovely and fair as the rose of the summer, Yet

'twas not her beauty a-lone that won me, Oh, no! 'twas the

truth in her eye e-ver dawning, That made me love Ma-ry, the

Rose of Tra-lee.

The cool shades of ev'-ning their mantle were spreading, And Ma-ry all

smiling was list'-ning to me, The moon thro' the val-ley herpale rays was

shed-ding, When I won the heart of the Rose of Tra-lee: Though

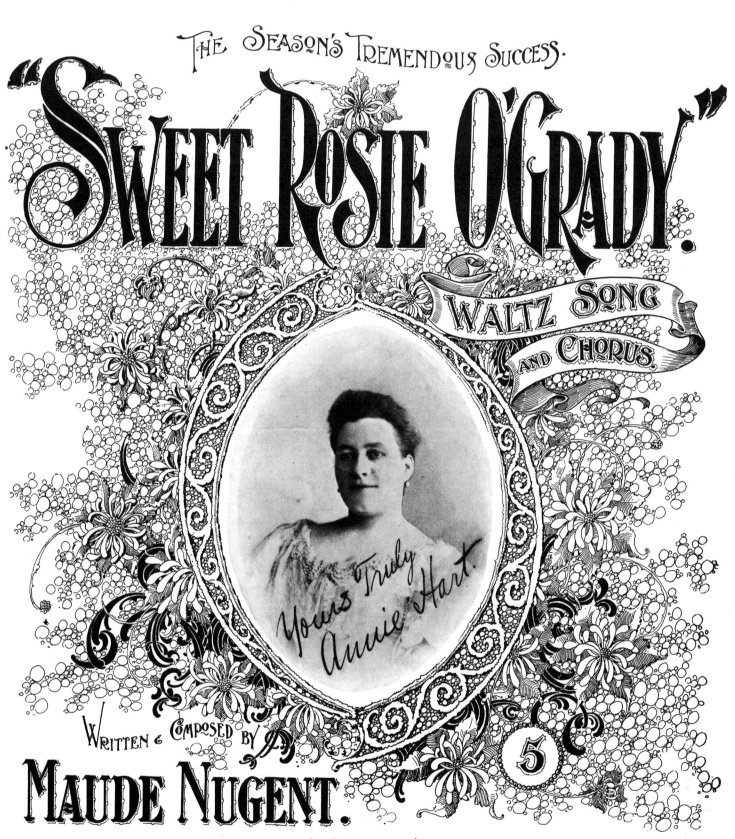

SWEET ROSIE O'GRADY.

Words and Music by Maude Nugent.

Just down a-round the cor-ner of the street where I re-side, There
I nev-er shall for-get the day she prom-ised to be mine, As

lives the cu-test lit-tle girl that I have ev-er spied; Her
we sat tell-ing love-tales, in the gold-en sum-mer time. 'Twas

name is Rose O'Gra-dy and, I don't mind tell-ing you, That
on her fin-ger that I placed a small en-gage-ment ring, While

she's the sweet-est lit-tle Rose the gar-den ev-er grew.
in the trees, the lit-tle birds this song they seemed to sing!

CHORUS. Valse.

Sweet Ro-sie O'Gra-dy, My dear lit-tle

Rose,⸺ She's my stea-dy la-dy,

Most ev'-ry-one knows,_____ And when we are mar - ried, How hap-py we'll be;_____ I love sweet Ro - sie O' Gra - dy, And Ro - sie O' Gra - dy, loves me. me_____

MAGGIE CLINE'S LATEST

COMIC SONG AND CHORUS.

THROW HIM DOWN McCLOSKEY.

WORDS AND MUSIC BY J. W. KELLEY.

HARDING'S MUSIC OFFICE

NEW YORK CITY.

"THROW HIM DOWN M'CLOSKEY."

(M'CLOSKEY'S GREAT FIGHT.)

Song & Chorus.

Words and Music by J. W. KELLY.

1.'Twas down at Dan McDevitt's at the
2. The fighters were to start in at a
3. They fought like two hy-e-nas 'till the

cor-ner of this street, There was to be a prize fight and both parties were to
quar-ter af-ter eight, But the na-gur did not show up and the hour was get-ting
for-ty sev-enth round, They scattered blood enough around by gosh, to paint the

meet; To make all the arrangements and see ev-'ry-thing was right, Mc
late; He sent a-round a mes-sen-ger who then went on to say, That the
town, Mc Closkey got a mouthful of poor Mc Crackens jowl. Mc

Closkey and a na-gur were to have a fin-ish fight; The rules were London
I-rish crowd would jump him and he couldn't get fair play; Then up steps Pete Mc
Cracken hollered 'murthur' and his seconds hollered "foul"! The friends of both the

Prize Ring and Mc Closkey said he'd try, To bate the na-gur wid one punch or
Cracken, And said that he would fight. Stand up or rough and tum-ble if Mc
fighters that in-stant did be-gin, To fight and ate each oth-er the whole

in the ring he'd die; The odds were on Mc Closkey tho the bet_ting it was
Closkey did n't bite? Mc Closkey says I'll go you, then the sec_onds got in
par_ty start_ed in, You couldn't tell the dif_rence in ㅅㅅ fighters if you'd

rit. *a tempo.*

small, 'Twas on Mc Closkey ten to one, On the na_gur, none at all.......
place, And the fighters started in to dec _ o _ rate each oth_ers face.......
try, Mc Cracken lost his up-per lip, Mc Closkey lost an eye.......

colla voce. *a tempo.*

CHORUS.

"Throw him down Mc Closkey," was to be the bat - tle cry,.......

f

Throw him down Mc Closkey, you can lick him if you try, And fu_ture gen_e_ra_tions, with wonder and de_light, Will read on his_t'ry's pages of the great Mc Closkey fight.....

(lively.)

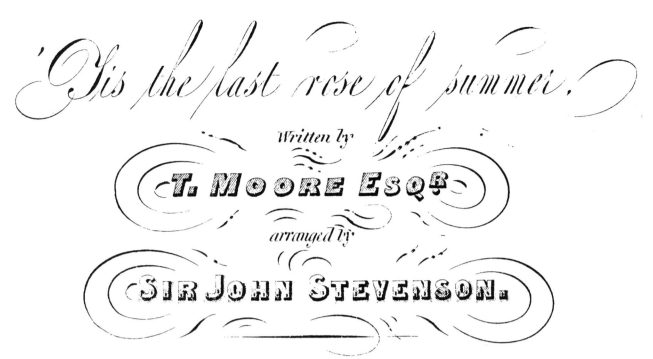

'Tis the last rose of summer.

Written by

T. MOORE ESQ^R

arranged by

SIR JOHN STEVENSON.

Published by **F. D. BENTEEN,** *Baltimore.*

W. H. DUFFY

PIANO.

'Tis the last rose of

summer, Left blooming a___lone, All her lovely com___panions Are

faded and gone; No flow'r of her kin―dred, No rose―bud is nigh,___ To re―flect back her blushes Or give sigh for sigh!

2

I'll not leave thee thou lone one!
    To pine on the stem;
Since the lovely are sleeping,
    Go sleep thou with them;
Thus kindly I scatter
    Thy leaves o'er the bed,
Where thy mates of the garden
    Lie scentless and dead.

3

So soon may I follow,
    When friendships decay,
And from love's shining circle
    The gems drop away!
When true hearts lie wither'd,
    And fond ones are flown,
Oh! who would inhabit
    This bleak world alone?

124   *'Tis the Last Rose of Summer*

TOO-RA-LOO-RA-LOO-RAL

That's An Irish Lullaby

LYRIC and MUSIC BY

J. R. SHANNON

PUBLISHED IN THE FOLLOWING ARRANGEMENTS

Vocal Solo, C–E♭–F–G . . . . *each* .50	Piano Solo (Gotham Classics No. 85) .50
Vocal Duet, E♭–G . . . . *each* .60	3 Part Mixed (SAB) 15
2 Part (SA or TB) 15	4 Part Mixed (SATB) 15
3 Part Treble (SSA) 15	Accordion Solo (Bass Clef) 50
4 Part Treble (SSAA) 16	Vocal Orchestration, F–C . . . . . . *each* .75
4 Part Male (TTBB) 15	Dance Orchestration (Fox Trot) 75
Band 1.00	

THE WITMARK BLACK AND WHITE SERIES

WHEN PERFORMING THIS COMPOSITION KINDLY GIVE ALL
PROGRAM CREDITS TO

M. Witmark & Sons

NEW YORK

Too-ra-loo-ra-loo-ral
THAT'S AN IRISH LULLABY

Words and Music
By J. R. SHANNON

simple little ditty, In her good ould Irish way, And I'd
hear her voice a-hummin' To me as in days of yore, When she

give the world if she could sing That song to me this day.___
used to rock me fast asleep Outside the cabin door.___

retard

retard

REFRAIN *Smoothly with much expression*
in time

"Too-ra-loo-ra-loo-ral,___ Too-ra-loo-ra-li,

mp in time

Too - ra - loo - ra - loo - ral,___ Hush now, don't you cry!___

Too - ra - loo - ra - loo - ral,___ Too - ra - loo - ra -

li, Too - ra - loo - ra - loo - ral, That's an I - rish lul - la -

1.   *retard*

2. Optional ending   *retard*

by."   loo - ral, That's an I - rish lul - la - by."

retard

Wearing of the Green

(an Irish Ballad of 1798.)

SONG OF

SHAUN THE POST

IN

ARRAH NA POGUE.

NEW YORK
Published by S.T. GORDON 538 Broadway.

3

THE

WEARING OF THE GREEN.

Song of "SHAUN THE POST."　　　　　　　　　　　　　　*In "ARRAH NA POGUE."*

1. Oh!
2. Then
3. But

Pad - dy,   dear,   and   did   you   hear   the   news   that's   go - in'
since   the   col - or   we   must   wear,   is   Eng - land's   cru - el
if   at - last   our   col - or   should   be   torn   from   Ire - land's

there's a bloody law a-gin' the Wear-in' o' the Green; I
'twill take root and flourish still, 'tho' un-der foot 'tis trod; When the
rich, and poor, stand e-qual, in the light of -free-dom's day; Oh,

met with Nap-per Tan-dy and he tuk me by the hand, And he
law can stop the blades of grass from growing as they grow, And
E - rin must we lave you, driv-en by the ty - rant's hand, Must we

said "how's poor ould Ire-land, and how does she stand?"
when the leaves in summer time, their verdure dare not show;
ask a moth-er's wel-come from a strange but hap-pier land?

132 *The Wearing of the Green*

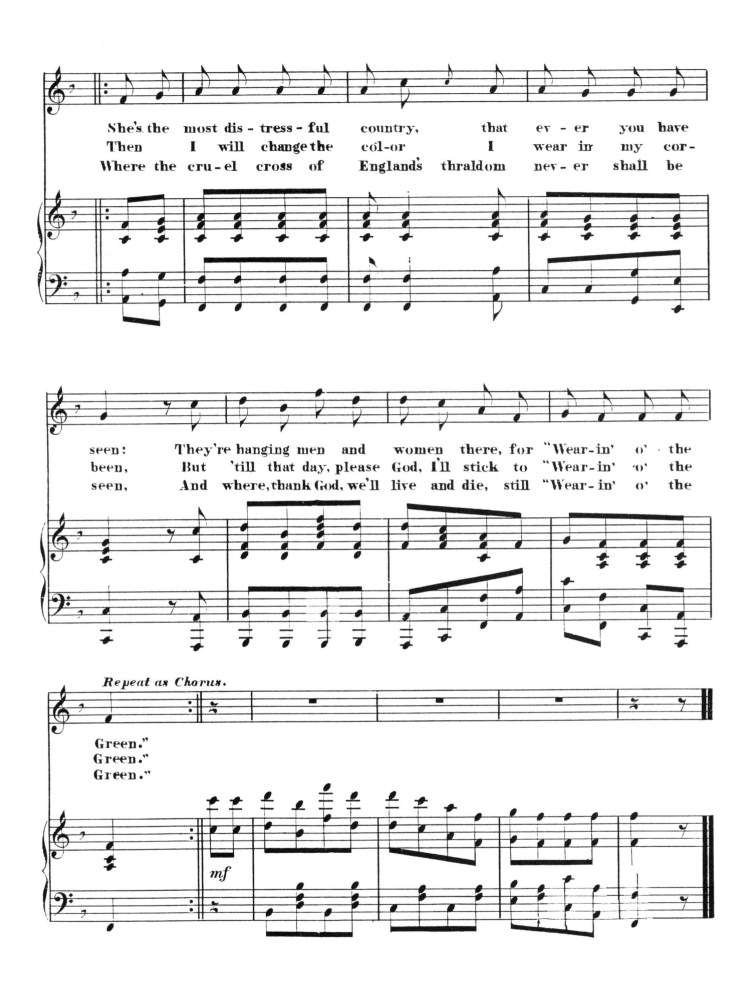

She's the most dis - tress - ful   country,   that   ev - er   you have
Then   I   will   change the   col-or   I   wear in   my   cor -
Where   the   cru - el   cross   of   England's   thraldom   nev - er   shall   be

seen: They're hanging men   and   women   there, for "Wear-in'   o'   the
been,   But   'till that day, please   God, I'll stick to "Wear-in'   o'   the
seen,   And   where, thank God, we'll   live and die,   still "Wear-in'   o'   the

Repeat as Chorus.

Green."
Green."
Green."

mf

When Irish Eyes are Smiling

Chauncey Olcott's

Song Successes

in his New Production

THE ISLE O' DREAMS

BY RIDA JOHNSON YOUNG
DIRECTION OF MR. HENRY MILLER

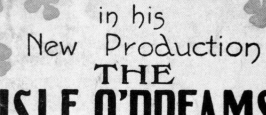

CALLING OF THE SEA, THE . . .	60
By Geo. Graff, Jr., Chauncey Olcott and Ernest R. Ball	
ISLE O' DREAMS . . .	60
By Geo. Graff, Jr., Chauncey Olcott and Ernest R. Ball	
KATHLEEN AROON	60
By Louis Weslyn, Chauncey Olcott and Ernest R. Ball	
MOTHER MACHREE . . .	60
By Rida Johnson Young, Chauncey Olcott and Ernest R. Ball	
WHEN IRISH EYES ARE SMILING .	60
By Geo. Graff, Jr., Chauncey Olcott and Ernest R. Ball	
INSTRUMENTAL	
SELECTION	1.00

M. WITMARK & SONS
NEW YORK · CHICAGO · SAN FRANCISCO · LONDON · PARIS · MELBOURNE

When Irish Eyes Are Smiling

Lyric by
CHAUNCEY OLCOTT
& GEO. GRAFF Jr.

Music by
ERNEST R. BALL

Valse moderato espressive

There's a tear in your eye, And I'm won-der-ing why, For it
For your smile is a part, Of the love in your heart, And it

nev - er should be there at all.____ With such pow'r in, your smile, Sure a
makes e - ven sun-shine more bright.____ Like the lin - nets sweet song, Croon-ing

stone you'd be - guile, So there's nev - er a tear-drop should fall.____ When your
all the day long, Comes your laugh-ter so ten - der and light.____ For the

WHEN JOHNNY COMES MARCHING HOME.

Words and Music by LOUIS LAMBERT.

1. When Johnny comes marching home a_gain, Hur_rah, Hur_rah, We'll give him a hearty welcome then, Hur_rah, Hur_rah; The men will cheer, the boys will shout, The ladies, they will

2. The old church bell will peal with joy, Hur_rah, Hur_rah, To wel__come home our darling boy, Hur_rah, Hur_rah; The vil_lage lads and lassies say, With roses they will

all turn out, And we'll all feel gay, When Johnny comes marching home.
strew the way, And we'll all feel gay, When Johnny comes marching home.

Solo.

3. Get rea _ dy for the Ju _ bi _ lee, Hur _ rah, Hur _
4. Let love and friendship on that day, Hur _ rah, Hur _

Chorus.

Solo.

_ rah, We'll give the he _ ro three times three, Hurrah, Hur _ rah, The
_ rah, Their choic _ est treasures then display, Hurrah, Hur _ rah, And

Chorus.

laur_el wreath is rea_dy now, To place up_on his loyal brow, And we'll
let each one perform some part, To fill with joy the warriors heart, And we'll

all feel gay, When Johnny comes marching home.
all feel gay, When Johnny comes marching home.

WHERE THE RIVER SHANNON FLOWS

SUNG BY JOHN RUSSELL

THE FAMOUS RUSSELL BROS

WORDS AND MUSIC BY
JAMES I. RUSSELL

M. WITMARK & SONS
NEW YORK   CHICAGO   SAN FRANCISCO   LONDON   PARIS

50¢
2½ NET

Where The River Shannon Flows.

JAMES I. RUSSELL.

fair - ies and the blar - ney   Will —— nev - er nev - er die.   It's the
bless the ship that takes me   To my dear old Er - in's shore.   There I'll

land of the shil - lal - ah,   My heart goes back there dai - ly   To the
set - tle down for - ev - er   I'll leave the old sod nev - er, And I'll

girl I left be - hind me When we kissed and said good - bye.
whis - per to my sweet-heart, "Come and take my name As - thore."

Chorus.

Where dear old Shannon's flow-ing, Where the threeleaved Shamrock's grows, Where my

heart is I am go-ing, To my lit-tle I-rish rose. And the

moment that I meet her With a hug and kiss I'll greet her, For there's

not a col-leen sweet-er, Where the Riv-er Shan-non flows.

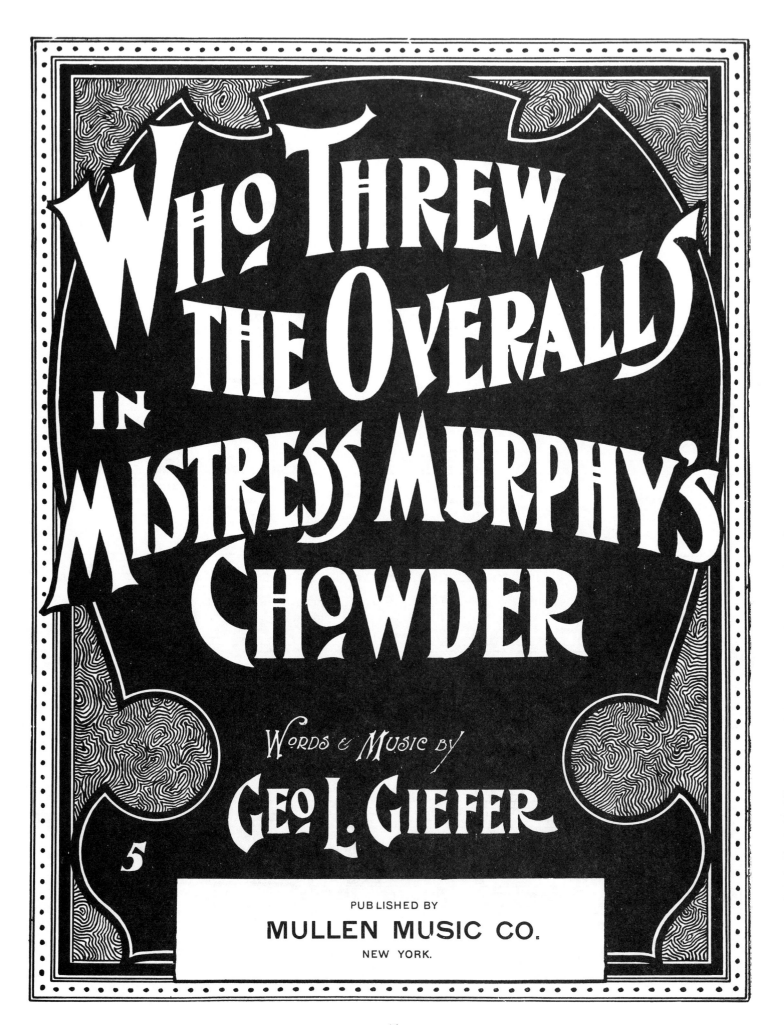

"Who Threw The Overalls In Mistress Murphy's Chowder."

Words & Music by GEO. L. GEIFER.

jumped up-on the Pi-an-o and loud-ly he did shout.
we put mu-sic to the words and sung with all our might.

CHORUS.

Who threw the ov-er-alls in Mistress Murphy's chow-der? No bo-dy

spoke so he shout-ed all the louder Its an I-rish trick that's true I can

lick the mick that threw the ov-er-alls in Mistress Murphy's chow - der